The Scarred Peach
Is the Sweetest

The Scarred Peach
Is the Sweetest

poems

Kathie-Louise Clarke

Chicago | Los Angeles

The Scarred Peach Is the Sweetest

Published in the United States by Match Factory Editions, 2026

ISBN 978-1-966253-25-9 (hardcover)
ISBN 978-1-966253-24-2 (paperback)
ISBN 978-1-966253-26-6 (ebook)

Library of Congress Control Number: 2025949618

matchfactoryeditions.com

Book layout by RD Morgan

Cover art and design by Gretchen Hasse

Colophon design by Randy Cochran

TABLE OF CONTENTS

I.

II.

III.

IV.

V.

I

My Life Is a Handkerchief

My life is a handkerchief folded into origami swans
by my family's complex love,
scrunched with tears,

washed by a tender mother,
pressed with my grandmother's dressmaking precision, and
patterned so richly by each joyous wave at a passing train.

Faded by each year turned,
frilled, and
feminine to suit my outfit,

squared ready for the fight.

I Am a Sticky Ball

Fragility is the sensation between joy and grief,
that rent of air when shrieks of laughter
fall into tears

so flimsy, gossamer
unable to weigh down the fluttering picnic blanket edges.

>   My father is shrinking in annual increments.
>   For years he took up space, but now his body is small,
>   better to blend with the birds he captures,
>   apertures open to just the right setting.
>   I hear the call of the Anna's hummingbird and need to tell him
>   the tiny peep-peep is calling me to him.

>   My mother used to knit sweaters to earn a little money
>   for luxuries, but the thick cables and beaded pearls of Aran yarn
>   were the purchaser's true indulgence.
>   I feel the rasp of wool as I dance the needles in and out,
>   over and under and over my fingers,
>   waiting for her guidance.

It is easy to weary of being the adult,
chasing blown paper down the street,
ignoring pennies dropped in a rush too hurried to claim them.

I am a sticky ball, rolling through life collecting people and experiences;
the colors simultaneously individual, and blurred.

My Tattoo

Blood blooms weeping
as I pick out the sutures, half healed scars
from your latest disregard.

Tears drip off your chin to pin the spotlight to my rivals,
the boyhood dream of the boy in the band.

I trace the constellation of moles from the peak of your ribcage
to the crest of your hip,
the strum of your heart my tattoo.

Bobbing along in your bass line with no one to see your face;
you lost me somewhere in the stage fog.

Time may have been kinder to you if you had stayed yourself
as you fall to your jewel toned knees,
bruised from all the times you should have held your backbone
in place of a stranger's hand.

When We Are Dust

Take that speck of dust
there, on the glass patio table;
that speck of dust belonged once
to the heavens, to the infinite stars
above our drip dried souls, to the trees
and the very earth that holds us,
binds us, one to the other;
specks of humanity loosened as we wring our hands,
at the pain of it all, but when we are dust,
and the trees still bear sentinel witness to the stars above,
we will have belonged, that is the hope of it all.

Fly Free

Sometimes flood uncovers treasure buried in ancient silt,
rageful tears lift years of burden, and
the cuckoo steals a nest to warm abandoned eggs.

Careless words sometimes open hearts with careful apology;
tired warriors lay their weapons aside, and
the scarred peach is the sweetest of a whole summer.

Sometimes joy finds the broken,
the failing are blessed with success
and the persecuted fly free.

Can we agree that beauty is in the angles,

the sight lines that snag on a glance and
hook on a briar patch of concern?

    Déjà vu,
          echo,
                souvenir,
all ways to dismiss growth as old wood.

When new framework rises from ashes, where
only the chimney stack was left to tell tales. Scarred brickwork
becomes a resolute foundation.

Now, do you see that dust explodes in sunlight,
blurred rainbow layers defined at the edges,
glitter as an armor of separation?

    Speck,
          mote,
                scintilla,
life's remnants are
left luggage with no chance,
faded ink the only sign it belonged.

Can we shatter this cynical yoke,
be dismantled, let shards poke and pierce,
be the parts of a sum?

    Revel,
          exude,
                embrace beauty in all angles.

Ruffians and Saints

Wouldn't we all be ruffians
if not for those saints who took the time to soothe us,
smooth us.

Inside to out is by far more vital work,
but to take this on alone is all but a fool's challenge. It takes fortitude,
moral strength, a faultless compass

to resist the ease of a quick flick of eyeliner
to shine up the suffering as growth, or the illusion of capability
woven by the slipping on of a fresh collared shirt.

To hold the bare bones and swaddle them, in muscles to be used for
virtue, veins deep with compassion and soft delicate tissue
as emotional absorbency, takes a saint's patience.

And yet this is the beautiful tension of ruffians who become saints.
The heart of the matter is shared and expanded to other rough hewn
souls in need of soothing, smoothing, building from the inside out.

The outside only reflects the best of the inside when it is worn
by another, a recipient of care, of generous love. The ruffles of a ruffian
smoothed, soothed, into a Saint.

You are the women

I'll leave my husband for at any hour
to share small sippy bottles of warmish wine
at the nail salon
where we air the bones of the day,
our rib cages open to freshen up our hearts.

If I find soup on the doorstep, I know who
cared enough to nourish me as she fed herself.
Sisters in soul,
each other's mothers/mothering each other,
the parkside leaves dance over us, for us.

Do not disturb does not apply to your call.
I will creep to the door in the dark to let you in
at any hour
and wipe your tears with wry solemnity
over the drama of keys lost to time.

When I need help to remove stains
of trouble past and searingly sound advice
on the calamity of being human—
you are the women, and
the parkside leaves dance over us, for us.

White Doves

To know we were not the same women as before did not pain us…

yet to say we have come to rest,
white doves on bowers of evergreen wouldn't do us justice

we have made endless drinks for men too important to recall our names

have earned degrees and honors and stretch marks and burns on the
inside of wrists from baking trays

born(e) children and weight no decent person would wish upon another

the Earth's core has shifted under us from despair to hope to hapless
denial of women's sovereignty

we knew ourselves then as we do now
capable, vulnerable, steady, wild, earnest, capacious, timid

and yet we are still a mystery and a danger to be contained

Bias Bindings

The curve of her neck as she dips to kiss our heads
is evidence enough that she is a willow on a windy day,
gentle, sensuous, taut wood under painted skin.

Ready to spring, snap back with resolve.
At the drift of her leaving we are left alert,
attention bound to the candid bias seams,

tenuous delicate stitches hold and
give with parting each step. Not a rustle or a strain,
but a pouring of skin and heart.

This day has worries enough of its own,
enough to blaze through the world in a fury of discontent.
Without the soothing glass of milk at bedtime, none of us will sleep.

Her marble hand will be busy rebuilding the future,
when we hear the Mourning Dove settle her feathers,
turning her pearl neck in a delicate curve to affix us with a percipient eye.

They left the floodwaters to rise, and her with no choice but to leave
the gown and the heart and the hand holding to others.
She is needed to pinch and pluck,

draw blood with tooth and crimson nail
for her place on the riverbank, in the mountain town,
the city hall, a world stage.

Snow-capped Goddess

The wanting wind caresses her poisoned heart,
encased in glass ribs, mountain high.
Beauty killed for spite refuses to diminish herself.

Manly princes climb the peaks on Odyssean challenges.
Wrapped in red and green, heraldic water-resistant suits
that only tears can penetrate.

They follow climber after climber after climber to take their glory.
Not one recognizes her majesty, her Snow White glow, and
the only ruby lips they kiss are those of fellow men in jubilation.

Dusted in ice-born glitter she lies, until finally the woman falls
to her knees and presses her face in the tender cold powder.
Thirst met with rewarding kisses down her throat.

Mercedes

a blow to the senses and sensibilities
indignation ignited by an overheard insensitive phrase

      heartsore that a marriage can become
            a post-it note on the cutting room floor of the
therapist's sanctuary

held together by salted slights deeply cut
and appreciation for abstract garden sculpture

when all else is bitter
sweetness lies in the refusal to
sell the car

II

Disparity Couplets

When an animal consumes its mate we marvel at nature,
but a woman must not demand too much of her lover.

At that we sigh, and label the partner's entrapment
desperate. We are duplicitous with ourselves.

Take the hard-shelled beetle, so black she is mirrored blue.
Her beauty shines dark and glorious,

recognizable throughout all insects as rare majesty,
but a dark-skinned woman is sold

and sold again, potions and elixirs to conform her
brow to paler tones, to tame her to a ghost.

So many creatures are adored in their voluptuous clothes of winter,
plump fur, curved breast and rolled neck.

They demand soft caresses and longing eyes, where their human sisters
would willingly wrap bone thin arms around them

for warmth, or drape them across razor blade shoulders
for elegance and plush youth.

The russet vixen, with steely gaze moves daintily across the snow.
Her auburn glow a warning that she accepts the wariest praise, but

only the bravest of men have seen the same beauty in women.
Painting tumbled ruby curls and luminous skin,

the models cursed as witches, bad luck, unnatural
bodies of a dark force, a blame for lust.

Divinations I

*"Live for yourself and you'll live in vain
Live for others and you'll live again"*—Bob Marley

Pull the cards and see what the future holds, unless
you don't believe and then it's just a story. A story
that may divine your path anyway.

Suggestion is a power unknown, just as courage
is a virtue, but carefully measured else it becomes
recklessness. Act like you already

have the virtues you want. Take the middle way,
the golden mean as per Aristotle's prescription
for a life well lived.

Travel from ancient Greece, to modern tarot via
the ruinously young Bob Marley, and
you may find truth.

Thirteen is a lucky number if you add the digits
one and three = four leaf clover, unless you are
Chinese and a'feared of the sound of death.

But what is death except a meeting with
the divine. Living in and with dichotomy, doing it all on
blind faith in a carefully measured

reckless act to feel joy, jaded sorrow, one for luck
two for a boy. Until you step on a crack or cross a ley line
and feel the divine shiver up your back.

Spy a black cat, eyes aglow with a joker's gaze
and know you are a Queen of Hearts transcending
the cards of fate. A little too much and still not enough.

Thoughts of the Milkmaid

Girl, you and that pearl earring,
it's all anyone sees.

You the luminous, enigmatic muse, the color of cherished veal,
promises staining your lips,
your essence preserved in oil.

Me in the same palate as you, with cupid playing at my feet,
my beauty unremarked upon.
I make bread and milk cows.

The painter gazed upon us and rendered your mischief inert, and
he ensured my drudgery would be eternal.
No wonder they call him a master.

Red Wolf I

When you come to me in the night,
hand across the taut sheet, I consider
waking.

My subconscious paints a picture in which you are
the wolf and I am cloaked in red. We writhe on this
bed.

As my hood folds back, you lose your
appetite and simper in apology
until I see your eye teeth.

To eat me whole you would have to
grow a stomach for difficulty, a gut
you don't have.

Entire worlds go by under my eyelids
and yet you are the wolf that stalks.
teeth at my throat.

I am tattered ribbons at your fingertips
and the wealth of Croesus is nothing
without love.

Red Wolf II

I'll eat chalk to make my voice soft and
powder my cheeks, wrists, and ankle bones
to fool you

once, twice, seven times a sinner.
I'll braid my red hair, curls tamed
taut to snare your tooth.

You can eat your fill of heartstones, heavy
with mystic power, gleaming from the
stream bed where fish swim free

over my lilied skin, my drawn hood tight.
But you won't consume me, because I was
never what you craved.

I was a bird, a centipede, a flying fox
above your head and beneath your feet.
Tying your laces to trip you

head first, belly aching into the well.
I'll spit chalk slowly and listen
for the depth of the drop.

His Words Become Your Feelings

In the beginning the knots give under his touch,
      firm blue threaded rope fingers work to prise
           strand
                from
                    strand
to gently tease the tension,
play with the slack,

until the ends lay loosely in his palm,
no more than strings.
But maybe even before that,

a lullaby carried through the alabaster walls
to root in the cellular sanctuary of a human skull.
A drum-beat of fingers on the sutures
trace for weakness
until
        his
        words
become
        your
        feelings.

Cut Scene

We came here to eat dinner but you can't swallow
your anger, it spills out over the table

like a delicate linen cloth,
we are gentle with the stitches, cautious of causing stains.

Lights reflect in the glasses, far more fragile than we have at home.
Fear of casual breakage makes our life utilitarian.

Voices of other diners, lovers and friends intrude,
providing cover for our rusted, grating conversation,

but you know I love you, and
you love a scene.

Can we leave before your wine becomes your reason,
before the server's tip confirms our shared guilt.

The rain pours over the canopy. We have shelter here, time
to take a breath as we wait for the cab.

Is it enough for you? Are you full?
Or should we try again with the leftovers.

Fireflies

Then again, I haven't seen fireflies—
and I believe they exist.

Plenty of times they have been jarred by a heavy hand
trapped; tiny pinpricks in the vast unvaried night
that fade at dawn.

While knowing this to be true and that to be false,
I have seen rabbits in puffed clouds chased by elephants,
faces of dead loves and fresh scars illuminated by Zeus.

Two dogs can lie quietly beside a fire, or sit attentive to command,
no compunction to self-improve. Languid cats can bask in the sun,
dreaming of birds in the shade hours of twilight,

and the hummingbird builds intricate teardrops to nestle their eggs,
beauty and purpose aligned. Insubstantial in conviction,
capacious in belief,

humans rely on angels to catch heaven-ward wishes,
seeking community like teeming fish in deep opalescent waves.
Won't you idle with me between now and that yet to come,

we can rest breathfully—be fireflies at dawn.

A Place I Have Been Is in Love with You

We entered slowly
along a white hallway
                 yet to be hung
with our memories.

Time gave rich tapestries,
plush rugs underfoot,
soft with understanding,
tiny flaws repaired.

Sometimes still I can enter a new room,
                           though less often now,
where there are treasures
to discover, packed away in tissue
to be revered,
held this way and that,
green glass with tiny air bubbles that catch the light.

In the attic I choose to hold you
and sip your scent,
each breath worthy of distillation.

III

Ancestral Web

For posterity and historical value you ask me to account for myself:

If I may be so bold as to imagine I sit in the middle of an ancestral web,
all threads mine to hold.
Are the outer edges my
mother,
grandmothers,
great-grandmothers a thousand times and more?

After-all, I was within these women since time was dust and
lizards stood to rule the world as men.

Could the outer silken strands be the lives of my daughters far beyond?
Dazzling in their astral beauty now that the planet 'home' is gone.

Is there a difference? When I can move fluidly across the filaments, to
gather and repair the bonds, the memories past and future.

Call me the spider then.

Easy in the cool shade of our mothers' labor for liberation:
the pill, homeownership, solo travel, divorce, choice. Comfortable
on the cushion of our grandmothers' war work:
land army, rations, painted smiles, lost loves. Reclined
on the ocean liner sized deck of our great-grandmothers' suffrage:
chains, hunger strikes, deportation.

Now I hold the matriarchs' baton in one of my eight legs, and this
present, this future, demands a precarious journey. There is little grace
for the clumsy.

Today we are possible

because the bees hurry
flower to hungry stamen
and cows shudder awake

we are possible, yet impossible, eyeballs
born the size of a universe, ears that grow eternally, and
hearts that meld into cynical defense.

Because birds wheel in the currents
above our concrete shells, our glossy heads,
while dogs lick our toes

we are possible, yet impossible, teeth that fall to be
nestled under pillows of slumber,
scented with hope.

Because I Fell for You

The bitter tang of your lips is the gin
to my tonic...

My tea-cup holds marmalade
I pour milk on my toast...
As I fall for you

I stare at my phone
your voice at my throat
my freshly ironed teeth chatter...
in wonder...
As I fall for you

I hear birds sing at night
and dream through the day...
As I fall for you

I sit in the river
my toes make ripples in the grassy bank...
As I fall for you

I am cast to the shore
you paddle away...
As I fall for you

A spoonful of sugar
stirred into the dog's dinner...
        I am making... of it all
Because I fell for you.

Self-portrait

It started with the taunt:
"Did you swallow the dictionary?"
My response: "Do you mean thesaurus?"
I licked the stamp on my fate with a sharp tongue
and sent myself to the side of the school yard once again
to be delivered as complete, thirty-five years later,
a word loving pettifogger with a penchant for
twisty meaning and obtuse facts.

      I am a poet.
I am not mean,
scared,
a bad mother,
without joy,
a skier,
without love,
a pessimist,
a joyful salad eater

      I am not
mean   with my time at least,
scared
      of failing—what is a path worth walking without a hill or two.

NOT a bad mother, it is worth stating twice.

Joy searches me out in the wag of a tail, a warm hand in mine, light on
the grasses by the freeway, a murmuration of birds, the ooze of warm
cookies. As to the rest, skiing requires too much equipment, love is
where you leave it, pessimism resides in salads.

Tragic Heroine

They are the generation that only knows what's breaking,
paint flaking, the *six feet apart but still in our hearts* sign one screw loose,
and yet we still remember the empty streets, the FaceTime calls,
the foggy masks, elbow bumps. It was going to save us all.

Now with the current flowing as it should, we stand knee deep,
cold white stones under our toes, to push feeling into our soles.
But what more can we do when God speaks to each of us as we are
made, carved, turned golems from clay, incarnated with love.

We hold fast to the illusion of control,
masquerading manipulation that means
we don't question the power to buy our way out.
Take a pill, chase it down with concern

that won't bubble up as bile but stay acid in your throat.
The universe started as Christmas lights, a nebula hung across the sky
showing the structure of a planet in ten million to call home.
Scientists tell us it is so; we don't question the pain man causes.

Through it all is a tragic heroine, a mother homeschooling while
judging the actions of the criminal, a sister wiping tears when
she too should be in school. A friend leaving soup on your doorstep
when all she wants is arms around her in connection.

Even while the cost remains unknown,
here we are, saved, on a sparkling cosmic bulb,
part of a string of celestial light so beautiful
even the scientists recognize it.

Illegal Knowledge

Is it a blessing when you are cursed with
swallowing obtuse, curious, eccentric, exotic nuggets
of tawdry, sublime, ridiculous, fact?

It's easy to weary of being the adult, arguing
every point one hundred and one ways, until the only point
is to teach a cautionary tale

against excess, greed,
tiresome pettiness of mean spirit, and cratered pores
filled with standing water of pungent despair.

To know you cannot refuse a stranger a glass of water in rural England,
or use of your Water Closet in Scotland, and to know hanging underwear
to dry in the sun on a Wednesday can bring the law to your door,

or to know prisoners shouldn't eat lobster more than three times a week
and one should never hunt moths under streetlights on Sunset Boulevard
gets us know-where

when only five percent of the moon has been explored. And children
pick through trash to feed siblings, and tired parents work three jobs
to eat Pop Tarts as a treat, when billionaires promise to give their wealth,

or eat it as lobster, with claws and all.

Too Many Cooks

Too many cooks spoil the broth, they said
as I sulked under the scrubbed wood
hull of the kitchen table,
the sails of gingham pooling
to hide my shame.

Cold flagstones smooth on the bare toe
peeking from the thick winter wool sock
my mother left by the hearth this morning
for my father, but he was long gone
into the blue dawn.

The skin of my testing hands
crackled as a cookie dusted with
sugar, as I traced the notches
in the totem legs of pine,
the four pillars of my new underworld.

Why must broth be the vessel
for misdeed,
that rich steamy comfort
tainted
by one touch too many.

Qualia of a Meyer Lemon

How we experience a Meyer lemon is different
from what the lemon actually is.

It is still yellow, and glossy,
and fragrant in all the right cases,
but the place in your tongue, and the part of your brain that knows,
knows that this is Meyer lemon, makes the simple citric acid
and white earth smell of inside the rind
less ordinary. Not a slice and ice sort of lemon,
but an artisanal jam type of fruit.

A prize-winning Dahlia the size of a dinner plate
would catch the gaze of all who pass, even if they are not humming and
buzzing in their fuzzy black and yellow dress suits.
The moment would be forged, agitated by the perception of seeing
something extraordinary; the heritage shades, the mix of regular, hearty
dahlias, would seem monochrome,
barely fit for an old milk jug on the kitchen table.

A sunrise cannot be seen as green, until it is in fact a mysterious
phenomenon, only available at a precise time, on a precise island;
the viewers' feet must be in the white sand, chilled toes dug deep
to hold on to the wonder.
To see the same sun rise over the same sea-lapped shore
on any other day is sepia, insipid,
not worth getting out of bed for.

Qualia lends the experience of the Meyer lemon, emotion despite
the rational knowledge, that lemons are lemons
are lemons; and

prize dahlias, though many petaled,
are no more worthy of an experiential moment of record,
than their vigorous weedy relatives; and the sun rises
and sets literally like clockwork, yet so few mornings excite us.

Desert Spring

I wandered into the doldrums
winding through sandstone columns of hope and regret—
        chiseled by my puckish nature

onwards I brushed past
arched memories
hand turned
as by the gentlest blush of breeze
to show layers of vibrant joy compressed in
Vantablack—empty of light

and there, glinting on the arid horizon a shot of tequila sang,
a cappella—
        my lament

one swallow would sear the tied cords of my throat
permit a voice once trapped to
      skip
           the umber

flit
—by cactus points of pain
cry-call to the dormant seeds
with breath misting out moisture
to raise up an army of wildflowers.

When We Were Wildflowers

You kissed me in the library,
delicate lips pressing life into my once dry leaves,
our held-back desire rustling pages and stirring dust.

Teen fiction and love poems,
tragedies and parodies laid as bare on the shelves
as our bodies to each other,

books so loved that they became mere bones,
newsprint wrapped. High shutters filtered light, glazing
your hair, kissing your shoulders.

In dusted beams, shadows danced,
lifted, swirled, and settled
in a puppetry of delight as fingers found new places to rest.

Glimpsed through the rows of fabric bound spines,
our love was green as spring leaves, though we lay
on ancient pulp fiction,

entangled wildflowers waiting to seed.

IV

Daughter of Gaia

I heard your sister got verdigris,
a lonely burden for one so sweet,
to carry the weight, a coastal rhythm night after day.
Salt-stained patina the surgeon can't remedy.

I dig through the sand that weights my heart,
see cobble stoned streets licked with a salted tongue,
and look to the fathomless/fathoms of ocean.
I don't want to share her sedentary fate.

Slick with the weeds of time
that resisted so many waves of fury,

I see her, daughter of Gaia,

calamitous,

        ominous,

                wondrous being.

A watery commander of the greatest swells/swelling,
the purpose of those held aloft and dragged ashore.

Wrecked by low tide, skeletal ribs of wood
stand proud/proudly showing the intransigence of man.
I know that to set forth to a new world I must
absorb the salted tears of Oceanus.

Bay of Dreams

Part I

Before he was a father he was a man of faith.
he could hold the lip of a fish to unhook it from pain—
without a tremble,
certainty giving a steady hand.
Yet when he gathered a wife
her wisps caught on his flustered fingers—
desire vaulted hurdles of reason

      to land softly

on the head of the newborn son,
which fit to his palm as a walnut nestles inside a shell.
One twist to the left would splinter the kernel.

When the boy broke free
each step without direction forged new hurt.
The tangents of carelessness
pulled threads in a deliberate world

      damage that moved from one organ to the next.

Dreams for his son appeared as luminous arches on the bay water
streamers of light gilding the boy in all his beauty
even as the shutters drew across his diminished soul
as a broken man of faith.

Part II

When Juan Carlos flew off the Golden Gate Bridge
                    into the bay of

            dreams
it was nothing more than a shipping channel
churned by a passing storm.

The international orange cage—solid
as the cell his father's tired soul—
fled.
A mother's grief clouded the sun that summer
until the waxing gibbous moon waned into the dark bay water.

His sister stood solemn eyed with marigolds in her arms
while the hungry tide licked her toes.
Each
            petal
                    she
                            dropped
for the foamy waves
declared the promise that she would hold her brother close.

Part III

Dancing on the uneven parquet floor
sprung to give bounce to her hair
she turned into the wide embrace of a rough cotton chest.

The scent of burden carried further that she had seen on a map
            assailed her
                    as the marigolds in her hair tumbled under his touch.

The baby was a boy
nutmeg in a fine down shell
all passion and warm spice.

She held his strong arms back from her breast
fearful of surrender
as he said goodbye.

The Mercy of Nereids

Let me place you at the ocean's depth

      my sisters sit on your chest
their whispers have drawn down a thousand ships.

Together we have wrapped your mortal bones with silken weed
the fathomless blue of our breath holds you
lips pale in the green light.

To find the loss you suffer
we search your silted pockets
but fifty nereids are no match for the deception of a human mind.

When you sought the monstrous Charybdis
and offered the last flashes of your
      sunlit
 soul

she spun with such vengeance
you wavered at the surface
the treasure of Gaia illuminated
in
      your final breath.

Ondine's Laughter

Over the surface of the lake skips a long-legged skater of fate
       half water, divided woman, Ondine,
           her sylph nature
               her mercurial form
captured in music for concert halls and open fields.
Turquoise tears slide over those who listen.

Her movements lithe, she prowls the willowed bank.
The dark lake does not satisfy her thirst for human connection,
settling moth-like on his aural glow,
her celadon eyes drawn to his grace—
       she cannot rest where she is not wanted.

The lightness of breath on his earlobe brings her into focus.
She moves languidly along the tranquil shore.
He takes one step,
         then two,
and feels his toes sink in the rich brown soil.

She lays back in the eddies, offers her silver fingers
to him. She joins the surface seamlessly,
no more than a sensuous reed resisting the current.
       He cannot take a hand he cannot see.

Rejection born of his mortal fallibility unleashes her
torrential   tempestuous
love diverted from purpose,
      each sparkling droplet
pierced with sorrow's arrow.
Her human form cries

              a frenzied soliloquy of shame.
Full rivulets of rain   streak his glass heart.

She is a marriage of fragility and strength,
          courage and madness.
                    Her laughter cleaves open the clouds of heaven.

Forbidden Kiss

Dusk falls quickly in the backstreets away from the shore.
Cobbled stones and tiles frosted with sea mist,
sweet summer days a cliche we have never known.

Our hands are frayed with the hauling of ropes,
but we wear the iridescent scales of countless fish.
We are clothed by Neptune's atelier.

Drawn to this when it's clear we shouldn't,
our bodies pressed to ice cold stone,
the kiss so fleeting.

The only sounds now the thrum of a motor,
gentle hiss of the waves on the harbor wall,
your quickened breath in my ear.

Our feet are wet from the depths of the ocean,
and we are damned by all three Furies
to wear the burning rags of guilt.

Safe Passage

Would that you could tumble in green waves,
be washed of all the mutated cells
in your heart, your brain, lungs, liver,
and surrender the searing
synapses to oblivion.

The deep ocean single cell bursts of light
may hurt your eyes, as they rise
to feast on all the pleasure
you can no longer see, tumbling as you are,
blind to the singular flash of sensation.

Beyond the tumult, past the deepest
hurt of the life not lived,
open trenches of sea feathered green
wait to caress the bones of you, to hold
and press you into fine white sand.

To calcify and reform your essence
into fossils for towering cliffs.
So risen to reflect the light of you,
luminous through the night to ensure
safe passage.

V

Ways to say; Plenty

: Trample : Peanuts : Bouquet : Wonder :
Full : Pernicious : Harvest : Enough

To have plenty requires us to trample over packing peanuts,
bouquets of wonder and full, pernicious harvests to be enough.

:or:

we could harvest each bouquet
      until our plenty full hearts, pernicious with lust,
         trample the peanuts and we cry

                            enough.

:perhaps instead:

We bow,
watching the elephant
trample peanuts
and taking deep
breaths of the
sickly bouquet
thrown at her feet:
white slipper petals
deep ruddy throats
with pollen that will create a stain
to last one hundred years, and
we wonder if it will have been enough

to have seen out
the pernicious

blight on the character
of the monkey in the
top hat
as he stands
whip in hand to harvest more
applause.

A Loud Silence

In the depth of my childhood home
a wood pigeon calls like no other:
"take two cows taffy"—

who are you though,
to be so demanding of neighbors
to take the soft hoo - hoo - hoo - hoo - hoo,
and join color with melody—

while its meaning is obscure to me
the repetitive demand soothes,
and I hear the call in the silence
when I am far from home.

A Triolet for the Morning Dove

We only need see the curve of the Mourning Dove's neck,
to know she is a willow on a river bank, ready to snap back with resolve.

The gentle reminder to keep us in check.
We only need see the curve of the Mourning Dove's neck,

her head soft against her breast, one eye closed, the other nutmeg.
She waits as we feel grief revolve.

We only need to see the curve of the Mourning Dove's neck,
to know she is a willow on a river bank, ready to snap back with resolve.

Bird Party

The wind rifles the leaves like a hand lazily stirring dried beans
setting in motion a kaleidoscope as they spin on the breeze.

Footsteps crunch the pine needles
        as popping candy hits a tongue.

The trees idle open with the squeak of an un-oiled gate
as sunlight kisses the dust shyly in parting.

This is the twitterlight, where white rush and silver rush
to arrive on time.

So many voices rise at once, discordant and symphonic,
        avian thrills over a tectonic beat,
                ethereal bursts of soprano layer
                    grandfatherly bass—

all hidden by reeds
on a lake shore sodden by rain.

Sol*ace

The New Year should have illuminated letters,
hand-drawn by ancient monks,
meandering wisps of incense,
highlighting its glory.

There is melancholic comfort in passing effortlessly
from one year to the next,
attending the mewling birth of a fresh start,
a zoetrope of promises to carry through the days.

Each new year should begin with a murmuring of swallows,
the swirl of feathers spelling

      HOPE

across the sky.

Solace is light
in the deep well of winter,
the solstice change from the longest nights,
to the brightness of dawn.

Remembrance Poppies

Slender neck
fragile bloom
      ruby

          paper

              thin

                  skin
anchored by wide fathomless eyes
open yet closed.

Now buried in fields far from home
awash on shores
fallen from the sky
given to sodden earth
hungry seas
cloudless nights.

Now crimson heads dance
brushed by a gentle breeze
keeping beat with nature
gossamer petals unfurl

      release their inward grip

              reach into
    the light

seeds ripen
    scatter

iterate the beauty of creation
        the symbol of the fallen.

Without Love

There cannot be grief without love.
No grief with tendrils that lap and curl
across the room, the country, the ocean mists,

foamy waves waiting to spread and blow across our view.
The last tomato of summer, the elderly pet fish,
the children of a country.

How else to measure these pains but by heft,
weighed in grams, bubbles, cries.
No grief to make everything become opaque, glassine. Beige.

In all of the ways we love and we lose, we have to love first.
The magnitude of love can be measured by the grief,
in fact perhaps that is the true definition of heft. Burden.

Love can burden us by the knowledge of grief
yet to come, anticipatory pain. Or worse, it's true
that grief can bring the realization of love, too late.

Boulders, pebbles, fossils of love we don't want to put down.
We are Heracles. We are Aphrodite in our strength of love,
our pained souls. We wrestle serpents and strangle ourselves

with unsaid feelings. We find a chick in an abandoned nest and want
to step in, meddle out of human born love. Then, we step over
a stranger curled into a sleeping bag and sigh at the messy grief of it.

This too is love.

Snowflake

In the half light of dawn
as a fractal/fraction of myself
I can't open my eyes
I am hard pressed
snow blind, as I become snow.

My world spins, spread out as the quilt I laid under last night
cocooned in comfort and flannel.

I fall sidelong
swirls of wind
blow each of my newly formed molecules
arranged in symmetry
unique and doomed.

Flurry/hurry
not alone, but lonely
multifaceted, the polymath I yearned to be
each crystal weakly bonded
refracts the early light.

Deep in my structure lay the minerals of a thousand years,
my knees in the morning used to tell the same story.

The heavens above
the tessellated city below
I can imprint my soul
on the hard tiles
or lay softly on the grass in surrender.

Light in the Mist

my phone camera can't capture what our eyes see
in the mist
luminous layers comfort the wet ground

dew drops lay
on leaves
like jeweled ladybird spots

once proud dandelion heads droop
their glistening teeth
curled inward

we walk past lighted windows
families at tables
couples in their kitchens

haughty cats
daring us to notice
their reflective eyes

headlights diffused to uselessness
bike lamps bob
like ancient trawlers in the bay

road barriers shimmer as they snake through the oceanic fog
looming dangerous
despite the safety they promise

the world is in greyscale
except at the end of the street
the one defiant red maple.

Notes

"My Life Is a Handkerchief" is written with a nod to Rafael Arévalo Martínez's line "I folded my heart like a handkerchief" in his poem "My Life Is a Memory."

"Fly Free" is a response to Sheenagh Pugh's poem "Sometimes."

"Ruffians and Saints" was inspired by "The Listener in the Corner" by R. S. Thomas.

"White Doves" was inspired by J. Mae Barizo's poem "The Women."

"Snow-capped Goddess" is about Junko Tabei, the first woman to scale Mount Everest, and Francys Arsentiev, the first American to summit Mount Everest without oxygen. Arsentiev died on her descent in 1998, and her frozen body, a waypoint for other climbers, became known as "Sleeping Beauty." The Nepali name for Mount Everest is Sagarmatha, meaning Goddess of the Sky. The Tibetan name is Chomolungma, meaning Goddess of the Valley.

"Mercedes" is after "Married Love" by Kathleen Flenniken and uses dialogue from a Post-it Note I once found in a stranger's house.

"Divinations I" uses a quote attributed to Bob Marley.

"Thoughts of a Milkmaid" is an ekphrastic for Johannes Vermeer's paintings *The Milkmaid* and *Girl with a Pearl Earring*.

"Red Wolf I" was inspired by Caroline Shea's poem "The Gothic Heroine Contemplates Murder."

"Red Wolf II" is a take on the fairy tale "The Wolf and the Seven Young Kids."

"Today we are possible" was inspired by Lucille Clifton's "birth-day."

"Because I Fell for You" was prompted by Nikki Giovanni's poem "I Wrote a Good Omelet."

"Too Many Cooks" was written after reading "Those Winter Sundays" by Robert Hayden.

"Ondine's Laughter" was inspired by Maurice Ravel's piano piece, which was based on Aloysius Bertrand's poem "Ondine" from *Gaspard de la Nuit*.

Acknowledgements

"I Am a Sticky Ball" was published in *Redheaded Stepchild Magazine*.

"Divinations I" appeared in *Teacakes and Tarot*, an anthology published by Spell Jar Press.

"Red Wolf and "Red Wolf II" first appeared in *The Orange & Bee*.

"Daughter of Gaia," "The Mercy of Nereids," and "Bay of Plenty" first appeared in *Seaside Gothic*, with my thanks to Seb Reilly for encouraging me to write more.

"Ondine's Laughter" first appeared in *Tiny Seed*.

"A Triolet for the Mourning Dove" appeared in *The Brussels Review*.

"Bird Party" and "Light in the Mist" were first published in *The Orchards Poetry Review*.

Gratitude is due to the editors of all of these publications.

"You Are the Women" was written for Gretchen Killion and Melissa Kellenberger—my women.

"Ondine's Laughter" wouldn't have been written without my hearing the music, played by the classical pianist Hunter Noack.

"Safe Passage" was written for my late Aunt, Beth Foxley.

Thank you to my fellow Chapbook Chamber writers who have become friends: Shymala, Allie, Ray, and Robyn—without all of you I wouldn't have believed I could get here.

Simon, George, Clementine, and Romilly—my darlings, my dears, my wonders, thank you for letting me force poetic thoughts upon you.

Thank you, always and forever to Lin and Martin (Mum and Dad)—literally my first ever readers!

About the Author

Kathie-Louise Clarke is a British-raised writer, artist, and Counseling Psychology MA student. She is inspired to create pieces that interrogate and illuminate the human condition, with a focus on love, loss, and the beauty of the natural world.

Since moving to California eleven years ago, Kathie-Louise has served in numerous volunteer capacities, taught herself Printmaking, started a business selling her artwork, taught Printmaking classes, and returned to writing. She is part of the Chapbook Chamber Collective, a small group of poets who work collaboratively to support one another and has been a regular host of weekly virtual Poetry Connected meetings (Monday Night Poetry Lounge) on Meetup.

Her poetry appears or is forthcoming in various journals including *The Brussels Review*, *The Orchards Poetry Journal*, *The Orange & Bee*, *Redheaded Stepchild Magazine*, and *Seaside Gothic*. This collection was shortlisted for the Longleaf Press Poetry Book prize.